bed

Georgia Gildea

V.

Published in the United Kingdom in 2023
by V. Press,
10 Vernon Grove,
Droitwich,
Worcestershire,
WR9 9LQ.

ISBN: 978-1-7398838-4-3

bed was selected and guest edited by Charlotte Gann as a V. Press Guest Editor title.

Cover photo & design © Sarah Leavesley, 2023
Printed in the U. K. on FSC accredited paper by 4edge Limited, www.4edge.co.uk/

Acknowledgement
The epigraph is taken from Louise Glück's essay 'The Education of the Poet', in *Proofs and Theories* (Manchester: Carcanet, 1999), pp10-11.

"The tragedy of anorexia seems to me that its intent is not self-destructive […] Its intent is to construct, in the only way possible when means are so limited, a plausible self."

Louise Glück, 'The Education of the Poet'

imagine a life pared down to a spoon
a frightened face bounced back

single image in
a bended mirror

what happens?
the outside disappears

and we're drawn into

bended image
single mirror
spoon

bed   the word hangs over my head

bed   a place to sleep

bed   the bottom of a sea   or lake

bed   a plot of ground prepared

       a supporting surface

       in case of emergency
       or breakage

bed   a heavy waiting list
bed   a national crisis

bed   upon or within which

                        a person

this is the part

where I give my name

but it's peeled away

like the *d* that's meant to be
on *ward*

war area
access to inpatients only

a door   a divide

where do *I* belong
my name
on which side?

                                                    I a suitcase
                                                    handed over

                                                    coat I won't
                                                    take off

                                                    I a goodbye
                                                    hug from my mother

                                                    I a room number

insert a collective noun
for *patients*

whisper? current? shoal?

patients

are a sharp intake of breath

patients cover up their mouths

never listen to music

theirs is a world
of absences

did I live
anywhere before this?

how can I find a way to speak
how can I know what is true
when this

other

has me in her image?

she
  wants to be
  an empty
  stem
  hang her
  bruised little
  head
like a bluebell

how can I begin
to lift my own?

the nurses say I need to talk

I *am* talking
all the time

questionsquestions looping
back unanswered

I talk myself into
my mouth

the space
of a suitcase

in which things have been (disturbed)
(uncovered) (overturned)

I talk   and it opens my underwear drawer
I talk   and it turns out my pockets

(stuff left rotting
blood in tissue paper)

once I have begun
to talk I find

I ~~can't stop~~

talk until my body
falls to pieces

the gardener unsettles me

white marks score her arms
gleaming as she reaches
for the shears

she was once
a patient here

and now
she's the ghost of all patients

lost ones who keep
coming back
to pace her tended lawn

mostly she works silently
neither here

nor not

I wonder if I'm imagining her

hunched figure deadheading
                    flowers

how old are we anyway?

we claim no adulthood
we're like

the hopeless collage on the walls

crêpe paper and cotton wool
limp sheep
under the giant lemon
of the sun

we are penned in

curdled in milk and juice
wrapped in pastel colours

                                        what *was* it
                                        out there
                                that frightened us?

I don't know where *better* is

or whether I want
to go there

setting off with nothing

except fear

it's like
          being made to leave

your home   with no

promise of another

knowing

your way is long

          and your tracks will disappear

I am walking into snow

a landscape of white static

white and muted

indeterminate

each forward step

undoes
a part
of the child
I never completed

making me scream
that I need to turn back
and retrieve her

  (grieve her)

and yet if I tried to give words to this grief
words would unravel my shame

(shame is scrunched up

mustn't be disturbed)

all I have   is the image
of a girl trapped   in another tense

pale
and reducing

to ash

when we want to harm ourselves

the nurses give us ice
tied up in a blue surgical glove

a disembodied hand to hold

we wring out its burn
picture smashed glass

pressed into our palms

it deters us only

because we are seen

as we feel ourselves to be

red-clawed and urgent hurting hurting

unable to point to the spot

I hear her in the shower
sobbing

her sobs run
under the door

the sound
of water over

fresh wet grief

the sobbing
and the running water

each becoming
the other

I've never heard
such

animal heaving
in the downpour

the trouble is
we fear   completion

imagine
it would end us

completion being
yes
a kind of end

completion is a rounding off
cue
for abandonment

we want
to keep pieces
in our pockets

to be forever owed

o

Jasmine
has giant eyes

a porous   way of talking
telling stories   from her troubled
life

there is so much Jasmine

she doesn't remember

how did she get here?

neighbours   a police car   doctors   hands

she's not like the rest of us

loads her cereal   with sugar   loads her mug
with hot chocolate powder   feeds distractedly

Jasmine is so full of gaps
she is open hunger

we watch and somehow
fear her

we whose borders   are *under control*

Anja is always
the source of alarm
in corridors

Anja who is otherworldly   silent

Anja   who won't lift her head
who whispers to flowers

Anja who comes suddenly
alive

throwing herself at the fire escape

bolting out of the garden

screaming
like a wounded animal

Anja

who seems barely there
Anja who is shadow

cries out in the corridors

for love

visitors arrive from where
we have lost our bearings

bringing smells
of wellness and creases

on clothes
surfacing pieces of context

because of the pressured present tense
we forget that we ever

had

brothers and sisters and mothers and dogs
worried-looking teachers

my brothers
are tall and handsomely made

all cheekbones
jaws and limbs

I watch as the young nurse
flusters and flirts

when
did they become men?

the dietician withdraws my milk
says I'm ready for

solids

striking through
another
fraught attachment

I was getting used to this
small and sipping creature

tended like an infant
tightly held

the dietician turns
her back

I throw myself
on the bed

(do I wish to be

beginning again?

yes
and yes
and yes)

outside is

a giant eye
too-dilated pupil

outside is an overwhelm
of light

I'm unselfed by surfaces

mirrors   windows   doors

I am shapeless
feeling   without form

I am context and its lack
an unbelonging
thing

I have lost
whatever
was holding me

am in danger   looping the grounds

is this the only illness that prefers itself to health?
that finds in all its symptoms

such seduction?

better
is a word

we blank over as we hear

distrusting its simple
offering

its judgement

to which side

does *I* belong?

on the bus to *meet some friends*
a walk-on part on the stage of their   fast lives

(I am so small
an aberration

clutching a strange name
flush with cigarettes
to stop my mouth)

they are
full of movement   mess and sex   forward-running
time

I hollow when they ask me

how I am

Lilian says there's *more to life*

as she watches us pluck at our cakes
while British Summer Time melts away
through pale curtained
windows

we sicken again at the word *more*
scatter handfuls of crumbs on the floor

more is what we're
terrified of

the vast
demand of being

saying *no* was a way of saying
I

and letting

nothing enter

a dark outline
holding *me*
together

no is narrow
self and safe

while *yes*
is open   other

yes
is frightened
yes

is large and hurting

no one prepares you
for the shock of

selfintheflesh

unprotected
screaming in the light

outside I'm
pursuedpursued

till I cannot stand

half collapsed
I'm rushed back

to their hands

all night is eternity

trapped between these
walls

all night I am watched into
my trouble

all night the nurse is yellow
light

and sometimes
a white torch

scanning through
this accident

or rubble

this is daylight windowsill   curtain morning bed

sheets and twisted limbs still
in the night

this is daylight windowsill

sweat and beating heart   pale blue   the shallows
of my breath

this is daylight windowsill   limbs still

in the night   this is pillow   this is bedside table
this is daylight windowsill   warm quilt over cold

this is never wanting   to unfold

after breaking
self is weak
quietly accepting

having nothing left
with which to fight

I let the daytime do its light
the day sounds
flicker through me

boat or bed

a small room
out to sea

we are not yet out of the woods
the family therapist says

we meaning *you*
or perhaps she's forgotten

my name

I for one have forgotten

can't tell if I
still have a face

what do people see
where *I* should be?

we are not yet out of the woods
meaning

cannot rest

whose woods are these
anyway?

why must I carry
the dark?

waking happens
gradually

and then
it happens fast

waking with this water
on my skin

waking in a sealed room
waking in steamed mirrors

waking from frozen
snow-filled years

the trouble
is the thawing out

the sudden
pain of skin

as if nothing
everything

(what happened)

this is the part where

  my life

is returned

with the other things I couldn't handle

  razors
  sharpener
  a pocket mirror

this is the threshold

these are the nurses
joking with my father

we hope we never
see you again

we don't step out into

a kinder world

or even one that's well

the air is full
of casual
little harms

don't listen

a game
of rock paper scissors

risk of

look ahead

being

cut up
flattened
overwhelmed

GEORGIA GILDEA is a writer from Oxford. She is a graduate of the Warwick Writing Programme and holds an MA in Creative Writing (Poetry) from Royal Holloway, University of London. She has published poems in *Marble*, *Lunate* and *The Cardiff Review*. Georgia is interested in writing that emerges from a place of voicelessness, and in the complex process of claiming a voice. *bed* is her debut pamphlet.